Poetry In Motion with Much Emotion
A Life Well Lived

Carol Ostrow

the three
tomatoes
The Three Tomatoes Book Publishing

Copyright © 2024 by Carol Ostrow

All rights reserved. No part of this book may be reproduced in any form or by any electronic or mechanical means including information storage and retrieval systems, without permission in writing from the publisher. The only exception is by a reviewer, who may quote short excerpts in a review. For permission requests, please address The Three Tomatoes Publishing.

Published June 2024 ISBN: 979-8-9903014-4-3

Library of Congress Control Number: 9798990301443

For information address:
The Three Tomatoes Book Publishing 6 Soundview Rd.
Glen Cove, NY 11542 www.thethreetomatoespublishing.com

Cover and interior design: Susan Herbst

All company and/or product names may be trade names, logos, trademarks, and/or registered trademarks and are the property of their respective owners.

DEDICATION

To my long-gone Aunt Tobi Diane Gruber,
a wonderful poet who taught me
the beauty of words.
I only recently appreciated her gift.

Author's Note

Words are so important. Remember: sticks and stones may break my bones, but words will never harm me? I think that is so wrong. Words express everything we think and feel. They lift us up and can be so powerful as to break us into little pieces. An actor can tell you how awful it is to read a terrible review about a part they are playing. Words can cause wars. Words can and are either weapons of destruction or can be used to show love, devotion and caring. They teach us all we need to know and guide us into our paths of living and learning. Words open the world to us, and we choose how to use them. Think about how politicians use words to persuade us to vote for them.

If you love language as I do, you choose words carefully as they are a reflection of you and who you are. That is why I love to express myself in poetry and use the rhyming technique. To me, they are like the lyrics to a song, propelling the story the playwright has in mind to the minds of those in the audience. Poetry is storytelling as Shakespeare and so many others have taught us. I am always telling a story, in my own fashion, in the poetry I have written for this book. I hope you enjoy it as much as I have experiencing it!

The Poems

Part 1: A Better Life 1

Permission 3
Looking At The Year Ahead.. 4
Survival Technique 5
Living In The Moment... 6
What A Way To Spend A Day... 7
The Day After Thanksgiving..8
Office Dilemma To Make You Shiver 10
Wear Your Best Coat 11
The Weekend Is For Sleeping...12
Words To Live By 13
Paradise Lost And Found 14
Living In The Moment..16
Simply Speaking 18
This Is What Happens When I Stay Home 19
Putting On The Breaks 20
Savor The Journey.. 22
Tough Day Today.. 23
Is What I Have Enough? 24
Thoughts On A Cold Winter's Day 26
Put It All Down In The Book Of Life 28
Lighten Up 29
This Is How It Is!.. 30
Just Get On With It! 32
Acceptance Of Change.. 33
A Gift Of Life... 34
Ah, The Simple Things 35
As The World Turns 36
Breaking Out... 37

Holiday Cheer 38
The Holiday Season 39
Nothing I Really Need To Do 40

Part 2: Appearance 43

Just Laugh At It All... 45
Save Your Money 46
You Have To Live To The Fullest 47
Stomach In, Chest Out 48
Don't Look Too Close 50
Birthday Thoughts To Share 52
Hiding Makes No Sense 53

Part 3: Self Esteem 55

Self Worth 57
Who Am I? 58
Never Give Permission To Take Away Your Power 60
Anger Is Seldom Poetic 62
Introspection 63
What Goes Down Does Come Up 64
Thoughts On A Spring Day... 66
More To Come Tomorrow 68
Decisions, Decisions! 70
Wake Up, Get Up, Move On!..71
A Female Dilemma Or Get Over It 72
Continuing, Asking, Feeling 73
Making Up My Mind 74
How Many Calories In Lettuce?..................................... 76
Give Yourself Approval... 78

Part 4: Friendships 81

You Are So Special 83
Thank You, My Friends 84
New Yorkers Are The Best 86
Your Choices 87
A Lesson From Me To You 88
I Went Home Alone 90
Getting Through It All 92
No Judgements 94

Part 5: Aging 95

Too Much Thinking! 97
An Uplifting Experience 98
Are You All Grown Up? 100
Am I Going Crazy? 102
Reality Check 104
Say It Again, Sam? 106
As Time Goes By 107
Experience Is The Teacher 108
Into Every Life 110
June 17th 112
A Paradox 113
Change With The Times 114
Is Time The Answer? 116

Part 6: Raging 117

Stand Together 119
Life And Death Decisions 120

Dedicated To The Brave Cassidy Hutchinson:
When You Know Something Is Wrong 121
Just Like You! 122
Hate Is Carefully Taught 123
The Changing World... 124
If You Don't Have Something Nice To Say... 126
What Century Is This?? 127
Take A Deep Breath... 128
My Mouth Is The Measure Of My Sanity 129
Nova Massacre Exhibit... 130
Let Freedom Ring... 132

Part 7: Love And Joy 133

Credit Where Credit Is Due 135
Being True To Your Own Feelings! 136
Rest In Peace 137
Don't Wait For Someone To Call You 138
Is Spring Really On The Way?.. 139
Memories Of Love 140
The End Of A Precious Life 142
So Be It.. 144
Memories Of Lost Loves On Valentine's Day 145
You Were More Than A Pet... 146
Feeding The Soul 147
Simple Pleasures 148
Not Always Of The Flesh.. 149
An Unexpected Encounter 150
The Joy Of Loving 152

Acknowledgements 155

About The Author 157

Part 1: A Better Life

PERMISSION

Today I am taking a day of rest,
Feeling guilty, of course, not at my best,
How could I dare be in bed all day,
Not being in the world at all to play?

One needs some time to shut out the phone,
To read, to write, to just be alone,
In a world that feels like a speeding train,
Where the news is upsetting, mostly a drain,

Why should I feel guilty shutting out the noise?
Usually, I conduct life with energy and poise,
One day without responsibility on my shoulders,
Where duties weigh in like large grey boulders,

Life will feel better, no permission to grant,
Tomorrow I will say there is nothing I can't,

Accomplish after a day of rest!!!!

Carol Ostrow

LOOKING AT THE YEAR AHEAD

Here it is, a brand-new year,
Quite different from others I remember so clear,
Praying to forget bad habits and fear.

Is the future full of longed for prosperity?
I do so hope, in all sincerity,
We simply survive!!
I'll be grateful, to just be alive.

Imagine in the not so distant past,
What we thought about, was just how fast,
We could eat, spend money, enjoy a blast.
Never dreaming that that would end,
That we might lose some family or a friend,
To a dreaded disease,
With such quick and quiet ease.

I am looking forward to a simpler life,
Less is more, without the strife,
And appreciate a little, to be sure,
Exactly what I am on earth for.

I am not looking for a new philosophy,
Or searching through the family tree.
Quite honestly,
I simply want to be,
The best person with the ability,
To bring joy as well as a bit of fun,
To absolutely every single one!

HAPPY NEW YEAR!!!

SURVIVAL TECHNIQUE

How am I now, much older and wiser?
Lately preoccupied with Moderna and Pfizer,
Still thinking of a bright future in sight,
After we get through this terrible fright.

Holidays pass too quickly by us,
Being with loved ones is certainly a plus,
Getting by is not the point at all,
It is filling a life this season, this Fall,
With faith in the fact that this too shall pass,
We will get through this with wit and some class,
Don't forget how to feel better,
One way is:
Find a person, go on and get her,
To give you some Botox and a bit of filler.
Feels terrific until you get the biller.

Oh, come on, at least get your hair done!

LIVING IN THE MOMENT

I think that spring is almost in the air –

Oh, just to have a day that's actually fair,
When I feel the warmth of the golden sun in my hair!
So, I can sit outside in a cafe, with absolutely no care
And hear the laughter of strangers sitting way over there,
At a table, eating, drinking, flirting, if they dare,
While I sit happily and comfortably
In a worn wooden chair

The changes in seasons are so disproportionate -
Cold weather in my bones makes me usually late
Since I pile on the clothes, walking slowly for a date,
While I wish I'd stayed home with a warm cuddly mate

However, when it gets so warm that I can't bear the heat;
Then, I long for my sweaters, with long sleeves to complete
The wardrobe needed for snow and wet sleet

Will I ever be satisfied with what I have at present?
I think I will since life, whether hot or cold, is rather pleasant.

WHAT A WAY TO SPEND A DAY

Reading a book was all that it took to make time fly by today

Getting into a story that had something to say
That's exciting, that feels like a play
That I might want to produce one day

It puts me in a delightful mood as such;
An important area in the brain it does touch,
As I love the feeling of turning the page,
Not sure if the emotion will be love or rage

It matters if the story does fully engage
My interest and full imagination,
As long as there is full integration

Then it envelops my life for that period of time,
And I don't want the story, exquisitely sublime

To end.

THE DAY AFTER THANKSGIVING

I am lying in bed on a holiday weekend,
Thinking of taking a walk with a friend

'No', I say, too lazy to move,
With absolutely nothing for me to prove

A few months ago, I was filled with a flame
To accomplish great deeds, many lions to tame

Life is different now with Covid to blame,
And I must live differently to feel no shame

In doing nothing in particular at present,
While still feeling good, to be content,
Regardless of what's happening in our world

Being now more mindful of danger out there,
To wear a mask to protect and care
About others besides ourselves

Forget about jewelry and clothes to wear,
As we learn what is really important, I swear

That I am going to live each moment
In the here and now and represent -

To be loving and thoughtful is all that I meant

To live here and now, not worried about what happens next.

Why I might even find a really exciting text
From a guy, I did not expect

Well, who knows what adventures will unfold!
I may have a terrific story to be told,

Right now, pulling the covers up, I am cold

Holidays are not always fun!

OFFICE DILEMMA TO MAKE YOU SHIVER

So, I am relaxing after three days of moving,
Thinking it could only be simple, proving
That I could do it easily alone

Ha-ha-ha!

After all, some furniture, a few pictures,
One phone, right?

Oh, what a mistake I made!

Should I call Medicare or Medicaid,
Before I faint and begin to fade?

The deed is done and I have to say,
Don't do it today or any day,
No matter what you have to pay -
Please, just, plain, stay

However, I have a feeling,
That by Monday, all is okay.

A good outlook keeps the demons at bay.

Oy Vey!!!

WEAR YOUR BEST COAT

If you live your life to the fullest, it cannot just be lived at home
You must get outside, as history has shown, into the world at large

Step outside

Do not hide

Or you may regret a decision unmade
To experience a moment that perhaps will fade
Into old age

Be a creator,
Come on, I met two husbands in an elevator,
Not at the same time, I might add

One was met at a party in a gorgeous pad,
The other was the path to a show business future

Well, that did not last too long
(The husband I mean for sure)
Just nine months cut and suture

So, what I say, these were life's directions I chose
It is wonderful to have these, them, and those,
To write about, tell stories about, and have great memories

Carol Ostrow

THE WEEKEND IS FOR SLEEPING

I think it's 8 a.m., or it could be 9 a.m. or 10 a.m.

Looking out the window, it's a wet, grey day
Should that determine what I feel or say?

Must that lower me into the depths of urban decay?

Decisions, decisions ...

I could resemble the weather, soggy and blue,
Or, summon the strength to paint a sunnier hue -
Or, choose to turn over in bed

I made the right choice, to rise up instead,
But not until noon, just to clear my head

I think it's Saturday, after all, so please, do not call,
Until late afternoon, when I am more at ease,
Since I require more sleep if you please.

Thank you!

WORDS TO LIVE BY

Get up, feel good, move on
Do everything while time hasn't gone
And left you in bed, with your imagination instead
Of doing what you've dreamed of in your head

Dreams, in fact, do come true;
These words are certainly not new,
So, take charge of your own steps,
Like building your strong biceps,
It requires picking up a heavy weight -

If that's a requirement, get it straight:
You are responsible for your own fate,
No kidding, my dear friends and mate

"Tomorrow is another day," you say?
How do you know you will stay
On the ground to move around?

You don't know what tomorrow will bring
Go now, be brave and do that thing
You have always wanted to do

Your friends will be there to walk you through -
Go on, do it now, just for you,
And stand tall.

Carol Ostrow

PARADISE LOST AND FOUND

I made a fast getaway to the Berkshire Mountain Range,
Only to discover an unexpected change

Nothing is quite the same, as I imagined in my mind
Since Covid, I sought comfort in dreams to find

Reality has set in, only a different kind

Nothing stays absolutely the same,
No matter who we seek to blame:

There are many changes –
It's a very different game!

Still, there's the sun bringing warmth to my face,
The trees bursting forth with life, swaying with grace -
Gazing into the green coy pond without a trace,
Of troubles that a vacation is supposed to erase

There are no troubles in Paradise,
Those are the ads, expected to entice

I'm certainly kept busy with exercise classes,
Supposed to round out my rather large masses
Of fat accumulated in the preceding year

This is where you come to hike and clear
The unnecessary inches on your old derriere

I choose the classes offered on a schedule

To get back into shape, eat food that will fuel

The future will be both kind and cruel

I love the spinning bike for an hour in the morning,
With cardio that has an ominous warning

This will be fine but don't overdo,
For too much of this can cripple you

So, on to a facial and a manicure at two,
Late lunch coming afterward, then, what to do?
Plenty!

LIVING IN THE MOMENT

If spring was a piece of candy, I would feast on its taste;
Not a drop or a morsel would I consider to waste

What a joy to feel the warmth, the kiss of the sun,
With longer days, enjoyed, as if the lottery was won
By a woman so happy to chase away the gray
Of winter's cold breath, easily forgotten today

So many books are written with recipes for happiness,
When it is so simple, like a breeze that will caress
An exposed part of the skin beneath a colorful cotton dress

The longed-for season's change, the azaleas in bloom,
The entire world looking up, instead of to Zoom –

The thought of nature coming alive, bursting from its cocoon!

These are just some of the ingredients to use
To come out of our shells and our lives to diffuse

A shocking, out-of-control year we have all lived through

With the vaccines, Broadway, culture to resume,

Grab it,

Enjoy it,

And fully consume,

Every minute as a gift you may assume
Will serve you as well as that yearned-for dessert

And go, with a mask, to that fabulous concert

You deserve all that there is to give and to get -
Please remember, never ever forget,
Life must be lived without a single regret

Well, at least for today!

SIMPLY SPEAKING

Seems that many have discovered joy in poetry:
A clever use of words written creatively

The rhythm, the beats, flowing meticulously

Put together to tell a story
Perhaps about personal love and glory
Or feelings, good, bad, or sad

Mine are momentary thoughts that must be expressed
Or would foment into a condition I might regret

Writing this kind of poetry,
Helps me feel deliciously free
To share a part of my history.

Try it, you might like it.

THIS IS WHAT HAPPENS WHEN I STAY HOME

Dorothy Parker wrote about love and stress,
A clever wit, not a famous actress

She often told us her penchant for Martinis,
And how they got her into bed with teeny weenies

I understand this out-of-hand dilemma,
With a light showing without all the glitter –

Just switch to wine; I do it all the time
And just fall asleep!

This I like the absolute most;
Then, my dears, I don't hump the host.

Carol Ostrow

PUTTING ON THE BREAKS

Wouldn't you know it, my phone's on the fritz,
Which doesn't allow me to freely kibbitz
With all my dear friends at home

Of course, there is another alternative I own,
But I'm using it now to compose this poem

We have all these gadgets to communicate -
It's the computers and Ipads that determine our fate;
Which I would choose to extricate,
Since they force my heartbeats to fluctuate,
When they don't seem to work anymore –

Frustration oozing out of every pore
Wait, dear reader, I have complaints galore!

I need some wine to calm myself down
Or take a short trip, perhaps out of town –

A clean, sandy beach,
But, not too far or out of reach,
Just in case I get no reception

On that damn cell, I need for connection

What, no WIFI? This could cause a conniption!

Don't people look insane? Most of them
Are talking on the street to a friendly ghost
With wires hanging from ear to ear,

Walking into traffic with absolutely no fear,
As they definitely cannot possibly hear
If a horn is blasting to warn of danger,
Which would certainly cause a rearrangement
Of their possibly mangled arms and legs

Oh well, if those people don't care, why should I?
After all, I've heard my phone ring while on the fly

Even in the elevator and I certainly tried
To have a decent conversation there,
Enclosed in that space without caring
Who was listening inside with me

Okay, lessons learned for me and thee:
Just please stop judging, we are all guilty
Of using our tech's capability
To the furthest reaches of possibility.

But, sometimes, it goes too far,
By the way, can I use your phone in the car?

Carol Ostrow

SAVOR THE JOURNEY

Non Illigetimi Carborundum,
Is the saying, in Latin, that is one,
Of the best sayings in all "Truthdom"

Don't let the bastards get you down
Get up, swim upstream or drown.

Come on, self-pity is a crying shame;
There is no guilt, absolutely no blame

So, you took a chance and did not aim,
In the direction of the prize, you hoped to claim

So, what!

Think of the Sinatra song,
"Dust yourself off and start over again"

Life, if you let it, gives you many chances
Take advantage of all new advances,
And, if you need help, just ask for it

No need to suffer, not even a bit!

Go on with your journey and do not quit:
The future is a jewel of a gift.

TOUGH DAY TODAY

Laughter is so good for the proverbial soul,
Especially when life feels out of control

Taking events much too seriously, you see -
I did not close a deal and had an extra fee
Tacked onto a bill most unexpectedly

I felt all my life's vulnerabilities,
Flashing before my very eyes
In a steady bombardment that surely defies
Twenty good years of psychotherapy
And felt deep pains in my lower extremity

"Where is that?" you may ask
Well, I'm trying to add some levity –
Touching on the border of bad taste

I think everyone needs a good belly laugh,
As I'm speaking on everyone else's behalf
Laughing at myself, of course, is freeing;
After all, I'm simply a frail human being.

Carol Ostrow

IS WHAT I HAVE ENOUGH?

What does it mean to have enough?
Is it a home brimming over with too much stuff?

Or, perhaps, that you have a large family,
With many branches on that particular tree?

For me, you see, it means something
Rather unexpected

It's hearing from a good friend,
A little laughter at the conversation's end -
Being able to see joy through pain,
Or a note from someone thinking
You would never see again

The surprise of finding a long-lost object,
Or hearing from an old boyfriend
Who is now single and asking you on a date,
And looking so handsome, you might consider him as a mate

This, my dear friends, you may appreciate:

It's the simple life that's really the best,
Although I do have a simple request,
To have a delicious meal and don't forget bed rest

As I am not looking for fame and fortune anymore,
Living a full life means being satisfied for sure,
With just getting up in the morning, saying hello to the cat

Believe me, right now, that's where it's at -
I am just so happy to be alive!

THOUGHTS ON A COLD WINTER'S DAY

I'm fascinated by the words we choose to express
Our feelings of joy, or the unexpected mess
We experience in minutes, seconds, or less
That happened like a flash in a day,
Whether at work or even at play

How in the world we can actually say
That our hearts are broken,

When words are not even spoken?

Language can be expressed through the flick of a wrist,
Or the head tossed back with a sudden twist

The eyes that lock on those of the offender,
That used to look soft and oh-so-tender
Now have degenerated into a stare,
And might be interpreted as a very sharp glare,

How difficult life can be when rage takes the offensive
But how delicious when you win your objective,
Just simply killing it with a look

Now, that's power when that's all that it took

However, best to never,
Lose your sense of humor

Be grateful, happier, not gloomier,

As someone can send a glance,
That will lead to your greatest romance!

I am ready.

How is now perchance?

PUT IT ALL DOWN IN THE BOOK OF LIFE

It is the Jewish New Year with so much to express,
It is the time to turn inward, to truly assess,
The year we have all lived through,
And what it all means for me and to you,

Have you given yourself to others in need,
Did you do something to halt sadness and greed,
In some small way did you do an unselfish deed?
Have you?
It is never too late to find someone to feed,

Write it down in your book of life.

One simple kindness can change us all,
Like telling a friend she looks pretty and so tall,
I love making memories of doing something nice,
Nothing huge which I find does surely suffice,

I have also done things I do not like much,
Now is the time to forgive with a light touch,
I am only human with many faults to forgive,
In the book of life, I will write how I want to live,

With dignity, kindness, giving more to charity,
Stop judging others, using much more clarity,
I will strive to be a more caring being,
In a world that has trouble really seeing,

That each of us is important in the book of life!

Write your own.

LIGHTEN UP

When I'm upset and holding back tears,
I hesitate to admit my innermost fears,
Holding back, perhaps with clenched fists,
Doesn't allow for unexpected twists,

Life, my goodness, as we all know,
Can change on a dime and will eventually show,
The sadness we feel now will evaporate in time,
The answers come without a whimper or a whine,

Have confidence, have faith with decisions made,
All the sadness will certainly eventually fade,

Remember, a sense of humor makes all things lighter,
Not always necessary to be a fighter,

You will survive,
It's good to feel alive!!

The sadness we feel now will evaporate in time.

Carol Ostrow

THIS IS HOW IT IS!

Just returned from an opera tour in Austria,
Thrilled to hear music, and many a famous aria,
With gorgeous scenery, fine wine and over fooded,
With every available luxury all included,
The days flew by filled with charming city sights,
Art Museums, dress shops, sampling dessert delights,
The city of Saltzburg bursting with curious tourists,
The joys of discovery that no one willingly resists,

Time goes by on vacation much too fast,
Must now pack up, get to the airport at last,
Discovering a peculiar feeling in the pit of my tummy,
Perhaps the excitement of leaving now feels funny,

Arriving early with a delay, there is some time to pass,
Delighted to have been upgraded to Business Class,
What luck I feel and prepared to now leave,
Then, the trouble began as I started to heave,

My body began shaking uncontrollably,
Was I reacting to something eaten turned rancidly,
Tossing, turning in considerable pain,
Hot then cold, too weak to complain,

Twelve hours later, home tested for Covid,
Sure enough, positive, waited for Paxlovid,
Lucky I feel to have survived this quest,
Now, liquids, light diet and much more rest,

This morning I began to read mail piled and stacked,

Only to find my bank account has been hacked,
Good Lord, is this some kind of test?
What a surprise I would not have guessed.

Oh well, I will deal with whatever comes to my door,
Just hope I catch the damned thieves before,
They make me completely and uncomfortably poor!!!

JUST GET ON WITH IT

What does it mean to have it all?
Do those words mean I walk straight and tall,
Even though, at the moment, I have hit a wall?
Sometimes I have to rise up after a bruising fall,

What do I do when frightened and in pain?
The reasons for this might sound hollow or inane,
As I put up a brave, secure image that's not true,
As I do not accept feeling sad or blue,

Having it all includes making mistakes,
Or how do we know without risking high stakes?
Is it alright to fail, start over again once more?
Does everything follow a pattern for sure?

The answer is, there's no answer for all of us,
Taking a wrong road can be turned into a plus,
Just get on with life and stop making a fuss,

Feeling alive means having everything!

ACCEPTANCE OF CHANGE

This time of year I notice colors are changing,
Coolness in the air is certainly rearranging,
All the excitement I feel in the days,
As I anticipate, suddenly, all the new ways,
I will wear my warmer clothes,
Miraculously my body senses and knows,
That darkness comes earlier now,
Nothing will be the same, somehow.

I will attempt to adapt without losing a step,
Grabbing hats, leather gloves, remembering to schlepp,
Probably an umbrella,
And an extra sweater,
Just in case my woolen coat gets wetter,
In the snowstorm sure to come.

It is very exciting to anticipate,
A new season with time to create,
Perhaps a fresh new idea,
Of course, I need energy to push away the fear,
Of realizing the passing of yet another year,
I do feel this allows me to be ever bolder,
Realizing,
For certain, I do not mind getting older.
However,
I just don't want to look it!

Carol Ostrow

A GIFT OF LIFE

I just heard of a friend who passed on today,
She was just here, only yesterday.

This is life and we need to appreciate,
How quickly it flies by. Is this our fate?
I look at my days, not shared with a mate,
So what if I don't have a Saturday night date?
Look at how much we all should be grateful for,
The sun is shining, or there's an unexpected downpour,
We have a little money to pay the bills,
Go to a movie for fun and some thrills,
A beloved pet who waits to be fed,
Or you have a person who won't go to bed,
Unless you are safely home... enough said.

How fortunate we are to just make simple choices,
To pick up a phone to hear welcome voices,
Let's be cheerful, joyful and most certainly careful,
Not to take chances with our gift of life full,
Of friends, family and those we love.

AH, THE SIMPLE THINGS

Today I am bursting with energy and love,
The warmth of the weather, a gift from above,
I need no jacket to keep out the cold,
In this climate, I will never, ever feel old.
The sun gives us strength to conquer, be bold,
It is a wondrous time, the truth be told.
Summer, and the living is easy, the lyrics say,
I believe those words on this beautiful day.
Won't you please join in, come out and play?

Honestly, it's time to be joyful now,
Get rid of that frown from your troubled brow,
The time is now, go and enjoy a new view,
The attitude of gratitude is all up to you.

Smile, love, live, and please call a friend,
This is truly the beginning, hardly the end!!

AS THE WORLD TURNS

I don't like being a victim of the weather.
You could have knocked me over with a feather,
When suddenly freezing outside as a measure,
That winter will soon arrive.

Does this mean that we'll be depressed,
If we have to be overly dressed,
In warm woolens to keep out the cold?
Really, that makes my bones feel old.

Ok, let's accept, that changes to expect,
When we look in closets to resurrect,
Everything we wore last year.
Let's look if perhaps a hole here or there,
To fix before we decide to wear.

Now, I look at boots, coats, a possible hat,
And hope and pray I did not get too fat,
To wear my black dress so comfy at that,
While zooming forever where I sat,
For hours and hours a day.
Okay I say.

This will not last forever!!
Let's remember that warmth will be back,
That moving around will pick up the slack,
And soon enough those clothes you will pack,
For the warmth of summer sun once again.

BREAKING OUT

Every now and then I want to burst into a song,
But, since I don't sing it would sound so wrong,
However, wanting to express feelings is very strong.

My own solution is to write a poem,
To share my thoughts with friends to show 'em,
(But, really, I'm saying what they already know),
That joy is expressed in a myriad of ways,
Like some clever people sit down to write plays,
That sometimes changes the world and
Stays,
In our heads for many years,
And may even bring us to tears.
This is why I am so grateful to say,
The lights are finally now up on Broadway.

How I missed the curtain slowly rising,
The music commencing with lyrics surprising,
Telling a story with a rhythm and a beat,
Losing myself in a tale so complete,
That I never even feel the cold or the heat,
Of the temperature of my own body.
That's so neat,
Don't you think?

Forget thinking. Let's just buy a ticket and enjoy!!

Carol Ostrow

HOLIDAY CHEER

You know what the best gift is this time of year?
I will shout it out so it's crystal clear,
It's a simple phone call to someone dear,
Just say hello, doesn't have to be Shakespeare,
Such a thoughtful, meaningful thing to do,
Makes a special hero out of little ole you,
Imagine the joy at the other end,
"Oh my goodness it's my darling friend",

That you took the time to think of them,
Frankly, it's worth more than a precious gem.

Isn't it the simple things that mean the most?
I lift my glass for a simple toast,
A Happy Holiday to you out there,
May this be the best, most prosperous year!

THE HOLIDAY SEASON

Now is the time for Christmas cheer,
It comes around only once a year,
It involves drinking champagne or even beer,
With a message that is so loud to hear,

The message that is so very clear,

Give gifts and tips to all who are near!
It might set you back financially here,
But, you'll do the right thing absolutely anywhere,
Do have fun, enjoy, because you really care,

And, I just want to be absolutely fair,

Enjoy Chanukah for all Jews everywhere!

Carol Ostrow

NOTHING I REALLY NEED TO DO

I love my weekends the most these days,
Slowing down from a time consuming craze,
Of packing in as much work as I can,
From Monday to Friday at the office to plan,

A life, a mission, proving who and what I am,

Ah, sleeping late, reading the Times in bed,
Thinking what shall I do, then turning over instead,
Of cleaning messy drawers,
Oh yes, I have plenty of chores,

Shall I skip the lunch I scheduled last week,
To go shopping at Ralph Lauren to have a peak,
At the gorgeous selection of the new season's dresses,
As that always releases the pent up stresses,

Yes, I think as the time goes by,
Getting out of bed to eat left over pie,
I think I will finish that exciting flick,
Picked out last week as a Netflix pick,

Getting so excited, lost in the film I chose,
It was Sunday morning by the time I arose,
To make more decisions about what to do,
With a free day to fill, not having a clue,

So, I will call my friends asking, "what's new with you"?

This is the best plan of all you see,

Without going on an expensive shopping spree,
I've rested, kept up with the recent news,
Talked to my pals which always tends to amuse,

By golly I'm exhausted, so before you know it,
It's Monday morning and, I'm hit with a bit of wit,

Thinking of what shall I do next weekend?

Carol Ostrow

Part 2: Appearance

JUST LAUGH AT IT ALL

I looked into my bathroom mirror and saw a surprising sight,
Who was that woman in natural light?
Could that be me that caused such an awful fright?
Why... yes... it was!!!!

I think I will need a forklift, as a facelift won't do,
As I studied the lines that were once so few.
What nature has wrought, so slowly too,
Has turned the picture into an entirely new view.
That I really had not noticed before.

This one-time Playboy Bunny centerfold,
Now has flabby thighs that support hose has to hold,
in place.
What happened to that once lovely, smooth face?
Today there is hardly a trace,
Of what used to be.

Right now just getting out of bed is a treat.
Receiving phone calls and something to eat,
Is the highlight of my day.

Although I can never be the former,
Spring is almost around the corner,
I can certainly look forward to warmer weather,
And enjoy life with my friends, altogether,
To remember:
That life is more than how you look,
Just think of all the adventures it took,
To get here in the first place.

There is nothing wrong with my memories!

Carol Ostrow

SAVE YOUR MONEY

As an actress over the age of 50,
It is clear a lifetime career becomes "iffy".
The camera, especially, doesn't love me anymore!
Even if my experience is better than before.

I started saving money for Botox and, for sure,
Every possible filler I searched to explore.
I found,
There are many to embrace and truly adore.
I have thought of filling every crevice and pore.

Aren't we allowed, as females, to get older with grace?
We must not live up to someone else's face,
As a few lines are certainly not a disgrace.

I am so grateful to be alive and well,
To move on in life with more stories to tell,
If someone doesn't think I look so swell,
Honey, you can go now, straight to hell.
Doesn't that sentiment ring your bell?

I just hired the bus...bye bye!

YOU HAVE TO LIVE TO THE FULLEST

Why, oh, why are my pants fitting so tight?
I woke up this morning feeling ever so slight,
Not having eaten a thing late last night

Why I even denied myself that cheesecake delight -
Not a morsel, not a taste, not a single bite, for dessert.

After so little I consumed at the table,
I tell you, it's enough to make me unstable

Do I have to consider running from midnight to noon
Or peddle my bike halfway to the moon
To use up calories that I barely consume?

Well, yes, that is the truth of food,
And the way it is used, but please do not brood

So, in fact, just look at it this way:
I promise you won't have to groan to display,
Your body in the mirror –

Turn only halfway!

For heaven's sake, you have lived this long;
Remember, a starving bird sings no song

Go ahead, indulge, don't be that strong;
You can eat without feeling terribly wrong

Take it from me, what I have learned this fall:
Just get a new pair of pants, slightly larger, that's all.

Carol Ostrow

STOMACH IN, CHEST OUT

Have you noticed?

Everyone looks like they're dressed for the gym
It's the same for the sexes, both her and him

Whatever happened to outfits by Lauren?
Or a snappy little number by Pierre Cardin?

Is this, in fact, why people get thin?

To wear tights that hold absolutely everything in?

I have gorgeous dresses in my closet,
Meant to be worn at the Summer's onset

Oh, well, I could make them ready to sell,
Call RealReal and have them tell,
If anyone's interested in Escada,

And if they are worth absolutely nada,
I don't really care –

I'll be myself in whatever I wear

Where is that old Gucci or Emilio Pucci?
OMG, will they even still fit me?

I have to grab those cute new jeans,
And not care what today's dress code actually means,
At least they are not bursting at the proverbial seams.

Oh, disregard those audible screams,
It's me, I gained 5 pounds it seems!

Carol Ostrow

DON'T LOOK TOO CLOSE

It's a gorgeous summer day and I wanted to think,
To sit in a cafe' with an ice cold drink,
To contemplate this crazy life I lead,
And decide what it is I really need.

Love people watching, it's a fun activity,
As long as it's not filled with any negativity,
I'm watching, judging and thoroughly engaged,
As the girls walk by in outfits cleverly staged,

The clothing, bright colors with greens and pink,
Some hems too high worn with heels that clink,
Good posture, chests out they're proud to show,
Graceful girls seeming to sway to and fro,

I'm not a girl anymore, no real complaints,
Just a little too many imaginary constraints,
What's wrong with dressing too young right now,
I feel young, carefree, not an old house frau,

Yet, I'm older than most of those l see,
The years have suddenly flown by me,
Where have they gone, what is left undone,
Has all been accomplished under the sun?

No, there is much to do to seek and find,
Challenges are there to tackle in kind,
I don't want to give up on knowledge to learn,
Self respect is still there to seek and to earn.

Growing older is a privilege not to regret,
Just wish it would slow down so I do not fret,
About the new wrinkles every day I get,
Every time I look in the damn mirror!

Carol Ostrow

BIRTHDAY THOUGHTS TO SHARE

I'm sorry to say that Mother Nature really sucks,
As now I need more nips and tucks.
Well... I used to have sex with men galore,
Didn't mind if they did drink or snore,
But ladies, I don't get asked anymore,
Good Lord, is it a nunnery I have in store?

I made an appointment for my shots of Botox,
And a long day prepared to put color on my locks,
So I can defy my age that's creeping up.

OK, don't get nauseous, I am simply being cautious,
In my new orthopedic shoes,
But today they are gorgeous Jimmy Choo's,
They don't chase away the blues.
However, I am determined in my skin,
To say to my friends and kin,

I feel good being just me,
I certainly hope you agree,
As all of you mean the world to me!!!!

HIDING MAKES NO SENSE

Although I'm not prepared to create a tome,
I thought I would take time to write a poem,
It is a tale similar to the late Nora Ephron,
Who wrote stories of truth we depended on,
Especially when she said she "hated her neck",
So, I decided, hey, what the heck,
And went to the surgeon with a hefty check.
Now, this was not an arbitrary decision,
It is serious and needed a careful opinion,
Requiring two or three or four or more.
It is not that I wanted to turn back time,
Who would I be kidding, it's so out of line,
It is simply for my very own well-being,
So that I can be comfy with what I am seeing,
In my mirror each day and can honestly
Say,
I will be the best looking gal in the retirement home.
I am not advocating for a lift and a pull,
Just not hiding a wish I can fulfill,
It's there for you, before you're over the hill.

Feeling good about yourself leaves room for better things.

Carol Ostrow

Part 3: Self Esteem

SELF WORTH

I have finally decided to accept and to own,
All the experiences, with my skills chiseled and honed,
The delights and the failures that reach to the bone,
That have made a person, in the flawed body, I call home.

I cannot change the person I've become,
I must accept myself, the completed sum,
Of the total parts that have made me one.

I've accepted the human being I put together,
From what my parents and teachers told me to measure,
To learn, to respect, to keep as a treasure,
All life lessons which taught me to measure,
Kindness, duty, to seek knowledge, to learn,
And, most importantly, to receive what I earn.
Eventually, perhaps sooner, it is also your turn,
To share this priceless knowledge:
That you are not entitled, this I can pledge,
To anything you did not earn,
This I can, from experience confirm,
No one gives you anything without a return.

What is it anyway, that's expected for a job well done?
Is it fame, a fortune or just plain fun?

I can tell in absolute full truth to be told,
I want to be proud of myself as I get old.

Don't you?

Carol Ostrow

WHO AM I?

Why is the myth of Wonder Woman so inconceivable?
Isn't being beautiful, smart and strong
Achievable?
I say yes in today's world of opportunity,
No matter a girl's age or born into ethnicity,
I am tired of the old rules on yellowed pages,
That define us with guidelines and expected stages,
Of a life's path to goals and gauges.

I'm creating a free life of my own choices,
That truly reflect my inner, healthy voices,
That guide the life I've always wanted to live,
With friends, family and much love to give.

To hell with what people think of me,
This life is mine, I think you'll agree?
I totally take full responsibility,
For whom and what I choose to be,
It is the same for you, don't you see?

Go on, risk, perhaps sing and dance,
If you don't do it now you'll regret the chance,
You did not take to fully advance,

This gift of life you were given,
You don't have to be sleepless and tirelessly driven,
Which is not an excuse to be rough and tough,
Because, we're fine, absolutely quite enough.

I cannot regret the long gone past,
It has flown away so very, very fast,

Come on Wonder Women, it's a metaphor,
To be who you are, right down to the core.

I want to say this as a fact and an admission,
You absolutely don't need anyone's permission!!!

I've had so much fun,
There's even more where this came from,
Thank you for your precious time,
For reading my poems in rhythm and rhyme

NEVER GIVE PERMISSION TO TAKE AWAY YOUR POWER

Today, my feelings were very deeply hurt;
I sought an opinion from someone too curt -
Someone who did not like what I had shown,
Suggesting my work was quite overblown
The approval sought, turned into a groan

Ouch!

Why do I need approval at all?
And why does it always turn into gall,
When not received, causing a serious fall
In my own frail, self-esteem?

What, in fact, does all this mean?

I reverted into a childish retreat –
Behavior remembered I tried to defeat,
With hard work and a therapist, for years,

Once a week!

And frankly, I hesitate to ever repeat,
And then feel empty, and then overeat

Yes, sometimes we fall backward like children

Well, so what?
Perhaps this is a lesson learned

Give no one the power to take away your fun
They cannot do it unless you allow it

I feel better now because
I ate only one piece of chocolate

Does this mean I am a grownup again?

Carol Ostrow

ANGER IS SELDOM POETIC

Tonight, I told a Maitre d' off

He acted like a pig in the proverbial trough

All I desired was a table, available in the center -
And he treated me like a village yenta

I told him very plainly that was oh-so-simple -
He was really awful — an annoying pimple

It made no difference, we sat and ordered our meal,
Paid the check, and I told that heel
We would never eat there again

I feel better when I express how I feel
Even if it is not so very genteel

Who says we should be ladylike and quiet?

Hell no, I say, let's defy it!

Of course, I do try not to be crass,
But, really, honestly,

He deserved a kick in the ass.

INTROSPECTION

'What is this life all about?' I ask in my head -
Not that I am contributing a thing, lying in bed

I really would like to do something instead
Is the answer in some book I still have not read

It's really an issue that I think I share
With all of you in the "great out there"

It's not a question terribly rare,
No, seriously, I do really care,
And am asking this question to actually dare,
To find an acceptable answer

Perhaps my purpose is to be on this journey
Where I will never know the meaning for me
But just keep going ahead, bravely as can be
In total mystery of where I am going and where I will land -

Simply learning, growing, open-mindedly
And realizing that the world does not revolve around me,
But around good friends and family,
With a little love along the way, most definitely

Better get out of bed eventually

Since today is Sunday,
And I need a little more sleep,
As these questions are a bit too deep.

Bye now: To be continued next week.

Carol Ostrow

WHAT GOES DOWN DOES COME UP

This evening, I feel so out of sorts -
Like playing tennis on quicksand courts,

I am sinking into a dark place fraught,
With imagined failings that amount to naught

Nothing is working; nothing feels right;
This means preparing for a tiring fight,
With just my feelings, within little ole me,
Like climbing to the top of an old apple tree

(Heavy sigh).

Nothing hurts, cannot take a pill
To remove the unrest since I'm really not ill;
Rising above this, requires some skill.

I do not have answers for why we feel blue;
It is probably natural, these days we go through –

So much uncertainty, our pleasures so few

Perhaps quietly, recognizing I cannot always feel well,
And not be ashamed to reveal my true self –

That is the way to real mental health

As Scarlett said, and I also wish to say,
Come on, tomorrow is yet another day

There, I feel better already!

(Deep breath).

THOUGHTS ON A SPRING DAY

No building has my name to commemorate my existence
Is that necessary proof of a good life, for instance?

However, it states that you have oodles of money

Is it satisfying enough to simply be here?
Let me just say, to be perfectly clear,
I'm happy to have a simple life of my choice,
Filling it with friends, culture, and work with a voice
That expresses more of who I think I am
Than bricks and mortar or even a video cam

Being famous apparently,
Isn't what it's cracked up to be,
As fame has its price,

Seems expensive to me,

I would prefer to come and go, feeling completely free
And stay out of sight, inconspicuously

However, I do feel that strange dichotomy,
Of wanting to dress up flamboyantly,
And be noticed and even admired at a chic party,
Or, if I find out that friends were invited without me,
It would turn out to my horror, absolutely ghastly

This my dears, sort of "Two Faces of Eve,"

Is what I truly believe:

I am a little bit of this and a bit of that,
As long as you never call me a spoiled brat,
I will be as happy as Nino the cat.

He loves me just the way I am!

MORE TO COME TOMORROW

I am looking back on my family history,
As I've always wanted a documented registry

There was beautiful Grandma, Jenny, on Daddy's side
With combined kids of nine to abide

They were bright, kind, with a dark and handsome look

My Mom's side had genius, red hair and that was all that it took
To give me an idea for my very next book

Do I go back generations to see what's in store?
Or do I look to the future and totally ignore
What I may not like to include in the lore?

There are secrets in all of our backgrounds, you know!

But each of us, during the years that we grow,
Are totally responsible for whatever we show
To the world

Haven't you heard?

Your life is your own -

From whatever seed you may have grown
You create what is outwardly shown

By the way, as soon as you realize this news,

Your history can really amuse
Anyone who might be interested

Big news ...

They are not!

Then you have the lighted spot
To make your life cold or sizzling hot

Come on, take your very best shot
The best was not yesterday.

Carol Ostrow

DECISIONS, DECISIONS!

Great people don't always think things out,
They may not have money nor any clout,
But they do go forward and will discover,
A new adventure, perhaps even a lover!

We know the untried road is really scary,
A wrong decision can get rather hairy,
Who cares if you fail, at least you've tried,
The truth, to confess, I've screamed and cried,

Why am I doing this, and, in retrospect,
I'm glad I did it with absolutely no regret,
So what, I say, pushing forward this idea,
What the hell, learning to live with constant fear,

Sometimes that works and sometimes it won't,
I'll never know if I stop and don't,

Move forward. You know what I mean!!!!

WAKE UP, GET UP, MOVE ON!

The end of an unexpected, exciting affair,
Trying hard to pretend not at all to care,
How thrilling it was to dream of togetherness,
Leaving only memories of lost tenderness,

It began quickly, with visions of a plan,
Moving in together, becoming my true fan,
A friend, then trust, then a wife I am,
Filled with love, respect and doing all I can,

To live the dream, well, it is only that,
When you find a fantasy is where it's at,

Thank goodness it was only a week,
As it started on a Monday, only to peek,
On A Sunday it was over completely,
Woke up the next Monday, new future to see,

It's alright to wake alone with just me!

Carol Ostrow

A FEMALE DILEMMA OR GET OVER IT!

My striving to reach a goal is insatiable,
Reaching the conclusion is quite probable,
The help to reach it is reliable,
But, am I really capable?

Who is judging?

CONTINUING, ASKING, FEELING

So what now will become of me,
Always associated with one or another he,
Nowadays realizing I am completely free,
Always adding another layer to be,

A fully realized and complete personality,

Will I ever stop asking questions?

Ah, that is the question!

Carol Ostrow

MAKING UP MY MIND

I do think my life is really happy,
Even though there's no man, tall and strappy,
To tell me how to live it, most surely,
Good or bad, left to my own thoughts purely,

Living alone, making all the decisions,
About where to go daily or making revisions,
Should I pay this bill or cancel streaming?
The costs so high have left me screaming,

What shall I cut out right now I ask?
At dinner shall I schlepp a wine filled flask?
Or take my own lunch to the office these days,
To eat at my desk, which is one of the ways,

To cut down on the finances I must raise,
I'm so not looking for anyone's praise,

It would just be nice to have a partner again!

Should I look for one of Society's pillars?
Would he object to my Botox and expensive fillers?
Oh no, I am not looking for his permission,
Certainly no regression into old time submission,

Still, wouldn't it be nice to have a fella?
As long as I don't behave like a Cinderella,
I can pay my own bills which is only fair,
It would simply be for him to care,

That we would make a loving pair.

I think I am going to risk my fate,
Shall it be Eharmony, OK Cupid or JDate?

HOW MANY CALORIES IN LETTUCE?

I have this annoying dilemma,
To keep my body fashionably slimmer,
As I age as gracefully as I can,
Is this the measure of who I am?

I exercise the parts that are thicker,
Concentrating on areas that are trickier,
I ignore diet pills offered on line,
The fads are empty promises to decline,

I search for clothes that reflect a look,
Taller, slimmer, as though that's all it took,
To look younger and fitter,
Forget the attention on glitter,

When do I just relax and accept my own body?
When I've lost 10 pounds and feel like a hottie?

My self-esteem is not related to weight,
Let's get this now and get it straight,

I am fine and so are you,
To thine own self be true,
This is definitely not a platitude,
Let's concentrate on an accepting attitude,

That we are terrific no matter our size,
Makes life healthier, and so very wise,
Let us decide now to actually devise,

A path to enjoy every moment we can,
Now, that is a much safer, saner plan,
Don't you think?

GIVE YOURSELF APPROVAL

I learned a lesson tonight, we all need to heed,
Which is:
We can get along, simply do not need,
Approval from others to win and succeed.

Last week I wrote a play, an original piece,
In rhyme and meter, a great challenge and release,
So much fun in the creation alone,
With no other distractions, not even a phone,
As the joy was there, just in feeling and tone,
Then, corrections, rehearsals with another actor in tow,
We were invited to perform in an evening's poetry show,
The audience on Zoom was engrossed it seemed,
As we acted the scene,
In pleasure and beamed,
At each face enshrined in their private screen,
While watching us.

Then, when it ended, only silence prevailed,
So quiet in fact I heard my breath inhaled,
What happened to the usual applause,
That is always given without a pause?

Nothing happened, no nothing at all!
Without a lost beat, my heart did fall,
This is in fact, an important lesson to recall,

In the future, let me never forget,
To ever depend on another to get,
The approval or love I seem to need.

May this sink in please, with all God's speed,
As I may forget it the next time!

Part 4: Friendships

YOU ARE SO SPECIAL

I'm writing to tell you how proud I am
To have you as my friends - So real!

This pushes me to be more than I am,
Never to be an "also-ran"

You are my chosen family,
Showing me how to be truly free,
Loving, accepting

Unconditionally -

You are so special to me!

Carol Ostrow

THANK YOU, MY FRIENDS

How will history remember this year?
Filled with terrors, errors and so much fear.
I will never forget the loss of my career,
That spanned a lifetime of laughter,
And sometimes a tear.

It went so fast.
Seemed like a minute, then became the past.

Is there a lesson to learn from all this?
What steps to avoid another sad crisis?
Can you hoard some form of happiness?

Yes....... At least I think we can.

You can choose to take a pill and chill,
Or, be of help to others who will,
Unexpectedly help you to gradually fill,
That awful void inside your head.
So, when at night, you take to your bed,
You are absolutely, completely exhausted.
Then, you are too tired to think so much.

Shopping, eating ice cream, are only
Temporary measures,
But hell, I love those fleeting pleasures.
Sometimes, that's all I have.

It's no sin.
That's where I have been,
Many times in a depressed state.

However, it is never too late,
To get out, exercise and speculate,
What your day will finally bring.
Hey,
Let's just look forward to Spring!

There really is no rousing cheer,
I will never forget this exhausting year.
However, I want to make it perfectly clear,
I feel better, bit by bit.
Very sincerely, I want to,
Thank you, dear friends who helped me, through it.

Carol Ostrow

NEW YORKERS ARE THE BEST

I had an accident this Friday at noon -
Flew to the ground as though on a witch's broom

I was dazed, almost crazed,
And blood flowed from my damaged brow bone

'How did this happen with my good balance and tone?'
I cried out, feeling so silly, bruised, and alone

Oh, the horror of landing on my face!

Then, hands on my arms lifted me to my feet -
Voices concerned, passing by on the street

Strangers asking questions, did I need some help?
Someone putting pressure on my open wound

Of this, I could barely make sense,
Until a kind man called an ambulance

All were people I had not met before,
Helping me, making absolutely sure
I was cared for before I was left on my own;
This was such kindness to a stranger shown

I thank you for your care to alleviate my pain
You, my saviors, never to be seen again

You are true New Yorkers I am grateful for this!

YOUR CHOICES

I do believe there are more good people than bad,
No matter the news we have recently had

The pundits make a living by spreading bad news;
That leaves us so sad and very confused,

However, my friends and those I'm surrounded by,
Are lovingly concerned and would always comply,
With kindness and respect that we give each other

This support, we share like a father or mother -
Even a big sister or very close brother

But this isn't what sells on Fox News,
As this is not the channel for us to choose

For grownups and me, I would rather see
The Times Magazine about sex after 70 -
Well, sex sells too, don't you agree?

Carol Ostrow

A LESSON FROM ME TO YOU

Writing poetry in anger leaves me no hanger
To store all this negative energy

Please, dear friends, forgive me

I turned anger inward where it grew,
Into something that is entirely new

It became an unwelcome depression
Where a frown became the expression,
That I showed to the world in dismay –

'Okay,' I say

This is the lesson I learned only today:

Never expect to be paid back
For a favor freely given
In love and respect
From generosity driven

That favor you bestowed was a gift,
Not to take back later on

This gift will cause a terrible rift
And a memory that saddens

Remember this lesson:

Giving without expecting anything in return,

Is a blessing that you certainly did earn

You will feel so good; for in the end,
This is worth everything, my friend

Surprise: your kindness is the only prize!

Carol Ostrow

I WENT HOME ALONE

Went to a party,
With all the glitterati,
And hoped to have a grand time,
Wearing an off the shoulder dress divine,

There I was in all my glory,
With not one person interested in my story,
It became very confusing to me,
When I spoke to a man who turned out to be,

A gorgeous hunk who's really a she,
Not that I care since it seemed clearly,
None of my business if she's a he,
And definitely not someone I'd marry,

I just wanted to have a conversation,
To make the evening a sensation,
As the room was filled to the absolute brim,
With actors and tall models so trim,

I wanted so much to fit in!

Well wouldn't you know it,
I dropped my drink on a poet,
Who stood beside me on the left,
He had this marvelous chin with a cleft,

It was love at first glance,
Even though I wet his pants,
With a gin and tonic with lime,

I felt in time he would be all mine,

Until his wife introduced herself!

I went home alone,
To talk on the phone,
With a caring friend,
Whose ear I could bend,

And had a fun evening after all!

GETTING THROUGH IT ALL

Some of us had an annis horribilis,
Suffering from effects of world craziness,
Many, mitigated the pain with some cannabis,
So what?

I, too, could have lived life fully stoned,
But then I couldn't have really owned,
The effects of a broken foot,
And a clumsy fall that actually took,

Me......completely and totally by surprise,
These occurrences actually opened my eyes,
To the fact, we really have no control,
When events then suddenly take a toll,

I did not cry or shout in pain,
As friends called again and again,
To hear my tales of woe so kindly,
Giving much needed attention to me,

I never received so much chicken soup,
From well meaning friends in my little group,
How could I complain,
When reciting a well known refrain,

"There's nothing like a good friend",
To get you through to the very end,
Especially when they complain and bend,
Your ears too!
No one is immune to accidents for sure,

The only remedy or even a cure,
Is to keep your sense of humor!

Promise!

Carol Ostrow

NO JUDGEMENTS

Well, guess what, it's really winter out there,
A snowstorm raging, perfect for a bear.
I am snugly warm, not moving from bed,
With problems swirling around my head.

Being a self-starter, feeling lazy today,
With certainly no permission to stay and play.
Solve one dilemma, then another peeks through,
Oh my goodness, too much to do.
Feed the cats, order food, walk to the office too,
Pay bills that piled up and magically grew.

Get up and go, with furry legs to shave,
What's the use, I can't even misbehave.
Have to get up, brush teeth and bathe.

Oh my, no energy to face what's to come.
I am turning over, reporting to no one.
Taking a nap, don't spoil the moment,
I'll do the same for you with no comment.

What's a friend for, right?

Part 4: Aging

TOO MUCH THINKING!

Lying in bed with nothing to intrude
Is not exactly euphoric solitude

I think of things that happened in the past,
That perhaps needed more nurturing in order to last

I am not reliving or rethinking another ending,
As that is a waste of time to be spending
On what I have done instead and pretending
That I could have prevented whatever happened

I could ask, 'Suppose I did this instead of that?'
This would lead to a meaningless chat
That would keep me up getting me fat,
As, for sure, I would crave la large piece of chocolate

Life happens, you make the decisions -
No time now for any revisions –

Relax, if you need help, a best friend will listen

You can call me, of course, anytime,
Would rather solve your problem than mine
Just do it after nine, please.

Carol Ostrow

AN UPLIFTING EXPERIENCE

One particular morning, just prior to the pandemic shutdown, I rushed out of bed to begin a really difficult albeit exciting day. I was going to produce a musical fundraiser for my favorite charity. So much to do, so many details to remember. I was anxious, well prepared and ready to go.

As I do every morning, I peered in the mirror to wash my hands, face, brush my teeth, doing all the normal, daily rituals. Then, quite casually, I looked closely into the mirror to insert my contact lenses. Suddenly, my jaw dropped. No, literally, my jaw line had dropped from a youthful oval to this rather unrecognizable square. Whose face was that looking back at me? I looked around the room. Good lord, it was me. I live alone.

I was much too busy that day putting the pieces together for the show to think about the shock of my aging facial features. Then, as we all experienced it, the Covid crisis took over our lives as well as serious political issues. I wore a mask, like everyone else and went about the business of survival, buying toilet paper and listening to the news. I even wrote a little poetry to keep sane. I did not think about my face.... until I did.

Now you know as well as I that make up and creams go just so far. I have so much filler and botox in me that if you turned me upside down, I would flood a basement. Nothing wrong with that and it works, to a point. That point was reached, and I made the decision to have my very annoying neck and jawline rejuvenated.

If you are considering this, please do your research, asking friends about the most popular surgeon is extremely important. Don't expect anyone to show you their own lifts, heaven forbid. Consultations are mandatory so that you have real expectations, not expecting miracles. I was astounded at the cost. It is equivalent to a down payment for a luxury apartment.

I found the most skilled surgeon, liked his realistic approach and made the date.

So, the decision was made, had the procedure and now following all the many important tasks in the day to a healthy recovery. I am very swollen, to be sure and uncomfortable, certainly. Very little bruising which is a welcome surprise. Giving up wine and caffeine was not as difficult as I thought.

I should be getting the stitches removed next week and ready for my appearance, in public, soon afterwards. Cannot wait to look and feel better about myself so that I can concentrate on doing good things in the world and not think about my appearance anymore. I just want to get dressed, go to work and enjoy my life and friends without thinking of how I look. Confidence is the real beauty treatment anyway, don't you think?

ARE YOU ALL GROWN UP?

Getting older is terrific but not an easy task,
You may have questions that compel you to ask,
Such as: do I still have a need to please,
Or just be me with long hoped for ease?

Can I now go online to find a main squeeze,
Will people call me a flirt and perhaps a tease?

For heaven's sake, when do we stop and grow up to use,
All the confidence we've earned to demand and refuse,
To be anyone else's idea of who or what we've become,
And ignore the nonsense of criticism that some,
Will whisper about your bold new self,
No matter what you do or say anyway.

Be you, the person you've become by living these years,
Of supporting, nurturing and surviving those tears,
By making mistakes, listening and surely learning,
To be the best possible person and absolutely earning,
Self-respect, love and never turning,
A deaf ear to those who need you.

Now, it's time to be free, give yourself an inner review,
Do you really care if gossip is about you?

Realize your dreams, it is now or never,
You can be smart and really clever,
By doing exactly what you want and,
Don't look back...... ever.

"Live the life you have dreamed of",
Said Thoreau, so purely full of love,
Stands true today,
Even better than in his day,
Get out of your own way.

Right now is all we have!!

Carol Ostrow

AM I GOING CRAZY?

Am I on a train going absolutely nowhere?
It is speeding along uncontrolled, I fear

Is it possible the future is really unclear?

And I have no idea how to break it down
Frankly, I feel like an old circus clown

Could time pass at a faster rate
Since I scarcely remember
The last meal I ate?

Today? Yesterday? or a further back?
Because it all seems to be the same

Can you, dear friend, plainly explain
What is happening, as I am in a bit of pain?

Aren't you?

Is the world going crazy, or am I unaware
That this speeding train we all seem to share
Is headed in the direction of what looks like hell?

But I don't know since it's damn hard to tell!

I fantasize all on board are eating
Chocolate bars in all the cars,

So that makes us feel we can all relate

To each other and our shaky future fate

Honestly, it makes more sense to me
That this road to hell is paved with candy
And my hero is riding on a white horse

Well, that's better than a train off-course -

Right?

What?
Crazy!

REALITY CHECK

All I want is harmony and peace -
This is not an excuse to create a speech,
But the result of a new facial crease

I swear I have looked inside to reach
Into an emotion that sincerely won't leach
From my intelligence

Nor does it drain from the relevance
Of the fact that I am happy to be older

It gives me the excuse to be bolder

Living in harmony is not about money;
It is making life lighter, perhaps even funny,

I need to find a way to mitigate
How I lost one inch in height that I hate
With the fact that I found four more pounds in weight,

Good Lord, is this my ultimate fate?

Well, frankly, I am going to be the best
That I possibly can be and finally rest
On the fact that I am not young anymore
And realize, right to the center of my core
That I love life with those I truly adore

Perhaps, l will finally embrace,
That I really cannot ever retrace,

The fresh look of youth –

Hell, to tell you the truth,
What I need now is a Dirty Martini with Vermouth!

What is your solution, I'm urgin'?
Don't tell me it's up to a good surgeon.

SAY IT AGAIN, SAM?

"Live the life you have dreamed of,"
Said Thoreau so purely out of love

That stands true today,
Even more than in his day

Get out of your own way.
The here and now is all we have!

AS TIME GOES BY

Sipping a Cappuccino in a local coffee bar,
A few steps from my place, really not too far,
Watching warmly dressed people hurrying by,
Wondering where they're headed and exactly why,

I sit here, people watching, while my life is on hold,
Am I wasting precious time as the coffee gets cold?
Worrying if life, scurrying by so fast,
Like one of the well-dressed girls running past,

The waiter warns me ever so politely,
The place is closing, please pay the fee,
I understand and certainly have plans to flee,
To the next appointment so important to me.

Is time spent quietly really a waste?
Must we fill up empty spaces with such haste?
No, not really, if it isn't your taste!

Relax and enjoy the moment. That is all we have.

Carol Ostrow

EXPERIENCE IS THE TEACHER

I have concluded it is time to give back at this age
I am old enough to have turned yet another page
To share what I have learned for another stage
In this short, last third of my life

Where did all the time go? I ask,
As I come to the end of another day's task

It has slipped by so quickly that I hardly noticed

Now's the time to share what I've learned
Or where is the pleasure of that which I've earned?

The wisdom, the experience must now be taught,
So that mistakes are avoided, the student not caught,
In a web of issues avoided, not fought

This comes with showing up, lessons learned -
I wish to pass on, my knowledge confirmed,
Through mistakes, corrections, coming out of defeat,
With head held up high, standing on two feet,
Steady on the ground, hearing a strong heartbeat

Is there a student ready to hear what I teach?

It would give me much pleasure to further reach
Out to that person willing to embrace
All I have to give - To share and face
The fact that this will be my legacy

To whom shall I bestow it?
This is the question I ask of you,
Perhaps you are facing this dilemma too

Tell me, please, your point of view:

I am listening.

Carol Ostrow

INTO EVERY LIFE

We simply do not get through a life
Without a little trouble, pain, and strife

Sometimes it pierces the skin with a knife

Hard to keep humor when you've fallen in the street,
And strangers pull you up to your unsteady feet

Yet, we gratefully thank our lucky stars,
When a doctor says there'll be no lasting scars.

We call our friends who listen intently;
Then, they kvetch to you rather intentionally,
Happy to tell you about their painful backache,
Or the details of an appointment they had to make
To find out why the antibiotic they take
Made their stomach upset and hands start to shake

Oh, my goodness, is this the start of a golden year,
When we're supposed to be happy, not shedding a tear?

Think of it this way:
Aren't we still here?

Thank you, Stephen Sondheim, for telling the truth
Let's celebrate with vodka and sweet vermouth

We're still around to laugh and complain
This life we live? Remember, it is not in vain,

It just comes with sugar and salt by the grain,

What doctor do you go to for that pain?
Call me tonight and once again,
Tell me what's wrong with you.

Carol Ostrow

JUNE 17TH

I lie in bed alone and hear a strange song,
No one beside me, is something wrong,
The melody, is it strains of sadness or longing,
Or the poignant echo of comfort and belonging?

I find comfort in my life at this moment,
It is filled nowadays with far less foment,
I close my eyes and relive the day past,
With those joyful moments that I hope will last,

Today was my birthday spent with best friends,
If this is my story, would this be how it ends,
With laughter, good food and birthday cake,
How simple are life's pleasures I choose to make,

Yes, I create my own story day after day,
Filled with many decisions and words to say,
Those words come to mind like a tape to repeat,
It's like a prayer of thanks for health and food to eat,

Thanks for your friendship, a gift you keep giving,
It's you my dear friends, who make life worth living!

A PARADOX

This is most definitely a statement, not a quiz,
The older I get, the harder it is,
To look and feel younger than my years,
Do most of you share these aging fears?

We wear more makeup to hide the lines,
Buying clothing that never really defines,
The year of our birth,
Striving to hide the extra girth,

That Mother Nature, that dictating witch,
Has given no choices to solve the glitch,

Of looking better the older we get,
I guess, in the end, we must totally accept,
Getting double doses of expensive Botox,
Or accepting the rather simple Paradox:

To get older......start thinking younger!

Carol Ostrow

CHANGE WITH THE TIMES

Shakespeare said, "all the world is a stage ",
For our modern times, TikTok is the rage,
No more books for our interests to engage,
It's the internet that entices instead of a page,

I'm a curious girl who loves a good story,
Remember the book, Tuesday's With Morrie?
About a lonely old man who outlived every friend,
Stayed wise and aware until his mortal end,

I love turning pages, the feel of a book,
Perhaps a story of how the earth really shook,
When a protagonist realizes a pretty female took,
His breath away with a sexy sad look,

Remember when we watched films in a movie house,
As hundreds with you were as quiet as a mouse?
The only sounds were crinkling bags of candy,
Or a laugh or two when the lead seemed randy,

Today we stay home to watch Netflix and Prime,
We even work from home so much of the time,

I've just made up my mind so you will see,
There is a place for all of us to adapt and be,
Old fashioned and modern, a mixture as we,

Decide to adapt or stay on the periphery,
The fact is it's quite the same quandary,
As I turn again to Shakespeare's, "to be or not to be",

I am a work in progress trying to keep up with change,
It takes so much energy to entirely rearrange,
The old world and the new one to fit my needs,
However, history shows that a little time succeeds,

In adapting all of us to change. But, do I really want it?
To sit in a cafe' with an ice cold drink,
To contemplate this crazy life I lead,
And decide what it is I really need.

IS TIME THE ANSWER?

It is a question of time:

Is it time?
Do we have time?
What time is it?
Isn't it about time?
You don't have the time,
Do you realize the time?
Take the time,
Her time is over,
We have nothing but time,
From time to time,
Time is of the essence,
He's doing time,

And then, no time to waste! Get it?

Part 6: Raging

STAND TOGETHER

I am searching for the words to express all the wretched feelings
And tremendous distress caused by the deluge of cruelty,
Exploding suddenly in my beloved city

Gathering momentum as a daily diet -
How did this happen? Who began this riot?
Women hurled to the ground and hit,
Boys attacked on the train where they quietly sit

The question is, how to stop the madness?
How to cure this rage that I must confess,
Has driven me into seemingly a hapless mess

I do not comprehend these acts of rage
That rate special attention on every newspaper's page
On all the media and every TV reporter's stage

Each of us must react and repel -
Never just stand by or hide from this hell;
If you see this insanity scream and yell
Or it will continue until, one day,
As history has repeatedly tried to convey,
You could become the prey
Let us be the ones who say, "No more!"
Do not be the one who closes that door.

Carol Ostrow

LIFE AND DEATH DECISIONS

Would I fight for my country's precious freedom?
Would I have the strength for the horror to come?

Could I handle the fighting and relentless pain,
With no food, water, or cover from the rain,
As those brave souls in all towns in Ukraine?

How I admire their fight to survive,
To keep spirits up to stay alive,

Could you risk your life, perhaps crippling pain,
Where you and family might surely be slain,
Without a whimper or a shout or care to complain?

Yes, God Bless America, to keep our Democracy;
It is the only place to live or die, for me!

DEDICATED TO THE BRAVE CASSIDY HUTCHINSON: WHEN YOU KNOW SOMETHING IS WRONG

When you have something on your chest,
And it causes pain with much unrest,
Think it out; do your absolute best
To find a reasonable solution

Take it from my own resolution,
To never, ever, be a willing victim!

It does not matter if you lose a fight;
What matters is that you feel right,
In your convictions and morality

You must separate the emotionality;
Get straight to the point with finality,
And don't dare go down silently

Shout out injustice and get all the facts straight;
Show up with backup, and do not be late;
Then, be confident and leave it to fate

You are a winner, never forget it,
No matter how the outcome will fit

You did not go down silently,
You are a hero to all, especially to me,

Thank you, Cassidy.

Carol Ostrow

JUST LIKE YOU!

Excuse me, Is this 1939?

A madman takes over a country by force,
Turning the entire world straight off its course

Watching brave Ukrainians defend fragile freedom,
As we watch every move on TV
From the horror of simple men, women, and children,
Huddled in dank basements and subways to hide in
To their brave leader announcing he will not run,
Pleading for his countrymen to pick up a gun

Those desperate to flee look back in sadness,
Dragging a few possessions on streets too dangerous –

Frightened, tired faces stained with tears,
Going forward despite their very worst fears

All they wanted was to keep a democracy,
To live in peace with friends and family

Beware! Now you can see how easily
This can be taken from you and me

It just takes a Putin or maybe,
A Trump who says he likes what he sees.

HATE IS CAREFULLY TAUGHT

I'm raging in sorrow and deep, dark despair,
Cannot turn off news streaming on the air,
Sleep is elusive with a sad broken heart,
What can I do, what is my part?

Let there be light instead of darkness of war,
But this isn't real til victims settle the score,
More horror and sorrow with hot flowing tears,
There must be a way to quell these fears,

Is peace a pipe dream that will not come to be,
In this lifetime for us and even our enemies?
Life is filled with such beauty and mystery,
This terror must stop being our history!

Carol Ostrow

THE CHANGING WORLD

The internet is driving me absolutely crazy,
Really, It's not because I'm suddenly lazy,
It's so difficult to remember 100 passwords,
And understand the X for new Twitter birds,

Or the absurd banking system of autopay,
And never hearing a human being say,
Not to worry, the problem is actually solved today,
I really feel it's a dark dragon to slay,

It's so hard to decipher the riddle of code,
My brain, every day is on overload,
Everyone I see is always looking down,
Thumbing out a message with a serious frown,

On the phone that no one uses to talk on!

Because there's no real person on the other end,
Unless the one you're calling is family or friend,
I swear, the world I knew is over and dead,
Now is the hour to take to my bed,

My hair is turning gray when once it was red,
From losing the position I held and have said,
Over and over how happy I once was,
Now my mind is filled with a disturbing buzz,

The old fashioned world, a simpler time,
Is over and definitely not yours or mine!
Oh well,

Forgive me, not to scold or harass,
Maybe we should take a computer class?

I

F YOU DON'T HAVE SOMETHING NICE TO SAY…

Words can be as dangerous as a sharp knife,
That will cut deeply into an unsuspecting life,
Choose carefully or risk hurting a friend,
That can be the beginning of a surprising end,

The repeating of gossip, not first seeming vicious,
Can be misconstrued, then, becoming suspicious,
Why was it repeated?
New thoughts added, inflated and heated,

I am, after all, just a frail human being,
Without training or knowledge of really seeing,
Why the person is spouting the nonsense,
It's repeating high school in the past tense,

I don't want to spend time on this anymore,
Moving past the hurt is surely the cure,
Love and respect will in the end endure,
Not repeating ugliness is best for sure,

By the way, telling the perpetrator off is very acceptable!
And you can throw hurtful words in the nearest receptacle.

WHAT CENTURY IS THIS??

How do I justify an old close friendship,
When she spouts political words that cruelly skip,
From one extreme to the other,
And ruthlessly seems to smother,

The rules of life I hold so very dear,
The rules of owning my body without fear,
That no one has the right to interfere,
With choosing my decisions, seems clear.

Does someone else rule over my body?

I thought that was between God, my doctor
And me.
I give no one permission to take my freedoms,
Or yours you see.

Carol Ostrow

TAKE A DEEP BREATH

Mental health is hardly a breeze,
With blasted nerves and all unease,
Surrounded by uncertainty in every day life,
What is the secret to assuage the strife?

I don't have the secret to calmness and joy,
If you have the answer, let me hear your ploy,
When I get anxious from live TV news,
And hear of war and the sadness it spews,

I change the channel before it takes a toll,

If only life had a remote control!

MY MOUTH IS THE MEASURE OF MY SANITY

I am in the habit of losing patience rather quickly,
Do the task fast or I become prickly,
Where is the joy in that my friend?
When, lately, I can barely run or bend,

Surely exercise and better food,
Will put me in a sweeter mood,

Hell, I've been denying myself sugar for so long,
That a little ice cream and sprinkles do belong,
On a restricted tongue that reacts rather strong,

To that marvelously cold shock of pleasure,
Beyond the usual daily weight that I measure,

To the taste of a delicious, creamy blend of glop,
Of chocolate, vanilla with a cherry on top,
The cool feeling on my mouth and teeth,
Gives me an orgasm felt way beneath,

My poor, sad neglected taste buds!

What did you think I was going to say?

Carol Ostrow

NOVA MASSACRE EXHIBIT

I saw the exhibition in a space on Wall Street,
Waiting for dear friends, with the purpose to meet,
To experience the event, for ourselves to see,
Putting together the pieces for them and for me,

Greeted with a fun musical film on a screen,
Gorgeous kids, laughing, innocent joy to be seen,

And then...the story unfolded, the reality too mean,

The rooms set up with small tents on either side,
The sandy floors covered with rugs to hide,
Any discomfort in a desert they might feel,
The sounds and the pictures amazingly real,

You begin to hear the rifles shooting into the crowd,
Screams, orders, hundreds running, crying so loud,
Suddenly, a video of a terrorist calling home so proud,
To say:
"Mom, I killed 10 Jews by my own hand today".

I see the table of shoes left behind in the crush,
The personal items, a small toothbrush,
The bodies of the murdered-on top of each other,
Terrorists screaming "God Is Good", smiling brother to brother,
As they look at the still warm bodies lying beneath a filthy, bloody boot,
And the entire world sends them more guns to shoot,

To these inhumane, bloodthirsty men,
That college students try now to defend.

If non-Jews do not stop this Hamas victim pretext,
For certain, you will be the ones suffering next!!!!!!

Carol Ostrow

LET FREEDOM RING

Writing for me is not a talent God given,
It is an aptitude that becomes functional when driven,
To escape the deleterious feelings that confront me,
With no other place to set and let free,
The damage that overwhelms from too much information,
Like a shooting, a killing somewhere in the nation.

Where are our leaders who can clean the mess?
All they do, I must confess,
Is confuse and twist, so a lie seems right,
Like a woman losing the important fight,
To control her own body that might,
Upset someone else's religious belief,
But, wasn't this country built as a relief,
From all that terror?
This is a grievous error!

Women, don't let this happen to you and your sisters,
Be brave, be strong, be the resisters,
Or,
We will all be back in the dark ages!!!!

Part 7: Love and Joy

CREDIT WHERE CREDIT IS DUE

It is said that women are the generous givers,
We give birth, juggle careers, prepare gourmet Chicken livers.
We nurture, care for family, keeping it all together,
Solve problems with a smile, through calm or stormy weather.
Do we get the appreciation we deserve?
Who is it that we really serve?
Honey, you need to pat yourself on the back!
Life is overwhelming, but you lead the pack.

On this Valentine's Day,
I will wholeheartedly say,
What you probably do not expect,
You deserve love and the greatest respect!!!

Carol Ostrow

BEING TRUE TO YOUR OWN FEELINGS!

I am listening to a moody love song,
That reminds me in words, loud and strong,
That love, that elusive feeling,
Is warm, joyous and completely healing.

It does not matter who or what you love,
Those judgements, disregard like an ill fitting glove,
No one has the right to critique your choice,
This is your heart that you give as a voice,
Loud and clear for all to hear and see,
To feel, to share, just there, to be.
Remember, I don't judge you, don't do that to me,
My choice is deep, remarkable, so truly free,
It does not matter if a She or a He,
Is the recipient of this gift you give,
It is a sign that you breathe and still live.

I want to live every moment!

REST IN PEACE

My darling cousin left this earth today
She was sweet, kind, and never had much to say

She was different from me, you see –

Wait! She was just here,
Only beginning her 77th year

Anya had a sweet face,
Never took up much space

I felt so alone, finding a resting place,
For her for all eternity

How short is our time on this earth!
With silly thoughts of the size of our girth!

How few are our years,if we fill them with tears!

Let's enjoy ourselves, as Anya would have wanted,
And celebrate life, the legacy she leaves.

Carol Ostrow

DON'T WAIT FOR SOMEONE TO CALL YOU

I want to tell you a simple story,
Not about bravery or stunning glory,
But about being thankful for living
And filling a life with giving

So, I called a close friend to hear her voice;
Later, called another simply by choice,
Just to say, 'Have a nice day;'
Then, dialed another friend to ask to play
Scrabble at our favorite restaurant – Okay?

She said, "Yes, I'll meet you in an hour or so"
I was clearly ready right then to go
But stopped to make yet another call
To a gal pal, perchance, to join us all,
Just in case she was lonely

I am telling you, there's no greater reward
That I hope you might hear and perhaps record:

People just want to be thought of, that's all -
Believe me, you will feel 10 feet tall

Go ahead, take time, make that loving call

You will never regret it, as it is to your credit,
That you took the time to think of someone else

Trying so hard to find a future plan,
We did and valiantly survived this 2020 year,
To live with hope and dignity to quell the fear.

IS SPRING REALLY ON THE WAY?

Can it be that the weather is actually changing?

That has affected my mind by rearranging
All my thoughts from frigid cold to warm
And enjoying nature's blooming in scent and form

When I shed the woolens, heavy winter's threads,
I notice more bodies, hands, and heads

Looking up is so much better today
Than lowering my face, keeping the cold winds away,
Protected from the damage they do in a day

I love the summer, anticipating the scents of roses in bloom,
Or the sweet smell of freshly mowed grass quite soon -

To be alive, to live yet another season,
Is such a gift and a wonderful reason,
To thank God, any way you are able

I will do it by bringing food to a dear friend's table

Perhaps rare cream cheese, lox, and the freshest bagel

Oh, for the simple pleasures in a complicated life!

Carol Ostrow

MEMORIES OF LOVE

Oh, how I miss being in love,
That surge of electricity that fit like a glove
Over my throbbing heart!

I remember my thoughts surging into another dimension -
Had to force my brain to pay attention

It felt as though I was falling over a cliff,
With an enormous wave of pleasure -
That loss of control, riding a wave one cannot measure

You know that familiar feeling:
Your imagination churning and reeling -

Suddenly, all of life is fun, so beautifully appealing,
Nothing's too difficult, the body's absence of pain,
And everything opens like a love song's refrain –
When there is hope, beauty, and so much to gain

I have felt this way in the distant past -
Where did it go? It traveled by so fast!

And it left me when I suddenly noticed
That I was alone, not really focused
On a partner in my head,
Nor a warm body in bed.

Life gives us many stages;
Our past has lived as a story on pages,
We experience choices, paths, and outrages

I prefer to remember the good times of it all,
But truly, the most exciting memory to recall,
Was locked in the tender arms of my man.

Carol Ostrow

THE END OF A PRECIOUS LIFE

Today, I had a terrible part to play,
That devastated me in every way:

The decision to let,
My darling cat, much more than a pet,
Live or leave this world,
As our lives together completely unfurled

While sitting in a room, alone together,
He, my Nino, light as a feather,
I was holding his precious body,
Reminiscing how he ran to me at the door each night,
Keeping me company or running out of sight,
To get me a toy to throw on the floor,
And play a game we came to adore

His coloring, a deep red fur coat, with almond-shaped eyes of gold
The brilliance of his mind, more than other breeds I'm told
He understood my needs, and if I may be so bold,
I loved him more than a human being!

Is it worth this sad and terrible pain?
What in the world do we actually gain?

A friend, a close pal, something to love,
A special gift from the Almighty above,

I had my cat for 15 wonderful years,
Now, my eyes are filled with sad tears,

Is it worth it? Yes.
Rest in peace, my darling Nino.

SO BE IT

I cried out in the darkness,
"Come and sleep with me!"
This, directed to my female cat,

Destri

I whispered so very seriously,
"You are my very favorite company"
"Come here", I pleaded, "for you can see,
I crave your attention most affectionately"

But maddeningly, she ignores every ardent plea
And chooses to slither away gracefully
To her favorite space to have a pee
And looks back at me rather haughtily,
To confirm, after all, oh so independently,
She's a cat after all and that is that!

MEMORIES OF LOST LOVES
ON VALENTINE'S DAY

I must have misplaced my heart today
Somehow it was lost, perhaps it flew away

Where did I put it?
Has it gone astray?

It was here just yesterday

In my thoughts of those years gone by,
When we loved so hard, you could hear a sigh,
Coming from a place so deep,
That remembering forces me to weep
Sweet tears running down my cheek

As I dream of you in my lonely bed,
You will always be in my heart and my head,
Even if other memories fade.

Carol Ostrow

YOU WERE MORE THAN A PET

I expected you to greet me today at the door
Then suddenly remembered

You are not here anymore

Do I remain sad or remember all the good,
That we shared and enjoyed whenever we could?

I know you would want me to be happy
And should go on with the wonderful memories we had

You made my life sweeter, and I am so glad
That we were together for so many years,
Although I am shedding all these sad tears

You are in heaven now with all your friends.
Thank you for making my life so joyous.

FEEDING THE SOUL

I awakened this morning in a cheery mood,
Trying to decide on choices for breakfast food,
Always concerned with consuming many calories,
Decided on an omelet with tomato and cheese,

I love walking into my clean little kitchen,
To gather ingredients and pans which in,
The imagination takes over, calories are fought,
I love creating dishes, to enjoy life as was taught,

By my wonderful father so many years ago,
Who loved cooking, knew of life's energy and flow,
He said food was not about nutrition as a goal,
Food is the way to nurture the soul.

Daddies know everything!!!!

SIMPLE PLEASURES

Love, it seems, is all around,
Even though I have not found,
The one!

Of course there have been a series of three,
Who were brave enough to marry me,
But now, the last one left me free,
All alone to simply be,

A woman, a person, to live and enjoy,
But all I want is a cute boy toy,
You know what I mean!
To bring me breakfast on a tray,
To do nice things for me each day,
To understand whatever I say,
Even when I refuse to play,

Any games, or call him nasty names,
When I want to be left alone,

You know what,
I'm living in a bubble,
A relationship is too much trouble.

Living alone is just fine.

NOT ALWAYS OF THE FLESH

Passion is a word I respect and love,
It is a feeling, a spark from high above,
Of nothing we can completely comprehend.
It is a flush of energy, a burst that may send,
A message to the brain of such pleasure,
even pain,
Containing all the things we usually constrain.
What a joy to feel that gorgeous surge,
To arise in the morning with a pleasurable urge,
To do that which gives so much in return.
Go forth, feel like a human who will sizzle and burn.
Like the bright and beautiful person you are.
Paint, write, cook, create a new candy bar,
What difference as long as you feel so far,
Alive with joy that nothing will mar,
To keep the fire of desire.

Passion, is never out of fashion,

As that feeling is a gift that keeps giving.

Carol Ostrow

AN UNEXPECTED ENCOUNTER

Yesterday was such a clear, lovely day,
Snow on the ground,
Melting all around,
That I felt in a mood to play.

Decided to get up and proceeded to dress,
Anything at all to relieve some stress.

Walked slowly to my favorite eating place,
Just to hear voices, see a familiar face.
I sat down, alone, to decide on a meal.
Given a menu of choices, omelets to veal,
Ordered a green salad with tuna fish,
Which happens to be the best brunch dish.
Then, of course, a Mimosa arrives first,
With a glass of water to quench my thirst.

Out of nowhere, in this outdoor hut of plastic,
Enters a man, almost a Tom Ford classic,
From the cover of Gentleman's Quarterly.
Not my usual type, quite honestly.
Blond hair, nice skin, rather fair and pale,
Looked rather handsome, an eight on the scale.
I took it all in, as you can certainly see,
While eating my food somewhat hungrily.

I consumed all on my plate, about to depart,
When a glass of wine appeared on my table.
An invitation to join that man, if I was able?
And that is the beginning of my personal fable.

I did sit down, had another drink,
Spent three more hours and did not think,
About chores, politics or serious business,
Just laughing, flirting, a glow of sexiness,
An ease with which I had not dealt,
Or frankly, the opportunity to have felt,
In such a very, very, long time.

What will happen in the future, who knows?
Is this a substitute for missed operas and shows?

Just a little fun to get the blood moving,
Which is, my dear friends just proving,

I am, indeed, still alive!!!

Carol Ostrow

THE JOY OF LOVING

The thing is, I absolutely love so many things in my life!

Actually, the things I love are not necessarily possessions, such as something tactile, that you can touch or even smell. That too, of course. They may be the color of the fallen leaves that have turned gold and red to remind me that winter is not far away. I love how the air feels crisp with a slight chill, reminding me to take out the warm coats stored in cloth bags all summer long, as well as the woolen sweaters resting so quietly, neatly folded in my bedroom closet.

I love to cuddle with my cat, Destri, in the morning when she quietly strolls up to my head just peeking out of a warm blanket in my bed, not quite ready to face the day. She gently rubs my exposed skin to remind me that she wishes to be shown affection and it is time to feed her. I pet her soft, black and gray striped fur, listening intently to her purring. She is the best companion and I love her dearly.

I love when the phone rings, at a reasonable hour, of course, and hear the voice of a dear friend chatting away about his/her activities for the day. I join in, so glad to have a schedule, interesting plans to perhaps see a brand-new Broadway musical that has had a buzz in the news and marvelous reviews in the Times. It is such a joyful feeling to have good friends and share information about our daily lives. I love that, even the non-hurtful gossip about who said what to whom.

I love the ritual of deciding what clothes to wear to the office that would have to be appropriate for any evening plans as well. Should I wear those chocolate leather pants I bought on sale at Ralph Lauren last year with a simple, beige satin blouse?

I love going to my favorite restaurants where the Maître D' knows my name. Then, after being seated at a quiet table in the corner of the crowded dining room, brings a glass of Prosecco to say thank you for my being there. My friends love this too. Who wouldn't?

I could go on and on about smelling the sweet fragrance of red roses in a bouquet received on my birthday or being pleasantly surprised by a letter from a relative who wishes to spend time in New York and would like to be with me. There is, after all, so much to love and be grateful for.

I do love my life and those I share it with. None of us knows how much time we have on earth. So, what I would like to share with you is: love every minute you have. As long as we have love, we have everything and that includes loving yourself most of all.

ACKNOWLEDGEMENTS

Can it really be four years since the pandemic took us by storm? How time does fly. Now, 2024, it feels like all of us have come out of the cocoon, unmasked and ready to live life again! I certainly am.

In 2020 my first book, POEMS FROM MY PANDEMIC PEN, was written and published by The Three Tomatoes Publishing. Cheryl Benton, the head tomato, had faith in me and worked hard to make the book a success. She and those who work for her are doing it again. I am very grateful!

My dear and close friends mean everything to me. I want to thank: Jane Goldman, Barbara Levey, Paula Novick, Jane Shevell, Julie Waslyn, Dr. Judy Kuriansky, Elaine Taylor Gordon, Margi Hirshberg, Glenna Freedman, Norma Feld, Shari Upbin, Arlene Herson, Sandra Maddock Schatz, Susan Shankman Banker, Lydia Sklar, Marlena Brauer, Gloria Dinsman, Revalee Brody, Howard Schraub and Sandi Durell of TheaterPizzazz for their loyalty and constant support. They read all the poems that I sent them, whether they were wanted or not, and always encouraged me to write more!!! I did. They are my family, and I am so grateful for their friendship.

I owe so much of my growth as a human being to the responsibility of being the President of the Actors' Temple for the last 10 years. Working beside Ben Sumrall our Executive Director, Rabbi Jill Hausman, assistant Cantor Aron Bederson, our Maintenance Manager Angel Villoda and the most wonderful, intelligent Board of Trustees anyone could ever work with has been an honor and a privilege. I also have to thank our attorney, Robert Reicher for never saying he is too busy to help solve problems. I could never have been the problem solver I have learned to be without this tremendous team effort. It is worth the aggravation and time!!

About The Author

Carol Ostrow is an accomplished theatrical producer in New York City. She has produced shows on Broadway such as *The Anti-Defamation League and Broadway; Hand In Hand Against Hate for 100 Years* as well as *I Am Anne Frank, the Musical* at Town Hall. She has produced many award winning Off-Broadway shows including *A Room Of One's Own*, starring Eileen Atkins, *After-Play* by the late great comedienne Anne Meara starring Jerry Stiller, and Rita Moreno as well as *Forbidden Broadway, Beau Jest* and many, many more in New York, around the United States and Europe.

For the past 10 years she has served as the President of the Actors' Temple, raised money for its renovation, creates videos and produced over 30 theatrical fundraisers and still counting. Carol also runs a licensed group sales ticketing agency for Broadway/Off-Broadway shows and when she finds the time, writes poetry for the love of words and all their meanings.

Made in the USA
Middletown, DE
01 July 2024